MAXIMS
Addressed to
YOUNG LADIES
On Their First
Establishment in the World

MAXIMS
Addressed to
YOUNG LADIES
On Their First
Establishment in the World

by
The Dowager Countess of Carlisle
1790

RAMPAGE
Distributed in the U.S. by Hippocrene Books, Inc.
171 Madison Avenue, New York, N.Y. 10016

Copyright © 1974 by Rampage Publishers

ISBN No. 0-914690-02-7

Library of Congress Catalog Card No. 74-81292

Published by Rampage Publishers, Danbury, Conn.

Printed in the U.S.A. by The Archives Press, Danbury, Conn.

Prefatory Note

In 1790 a small book with minuscule type was published in Philadelphia, by William Spotswood, entitled *Rudiments of Taste, in a Series of Letters from a Mother to Her Daughter,* by one Mrs. Peddle. The gush of her prose was virtually uncontained. The effects upon the daughter cannot be told.

The second part of the volume was called *Maxims Addressed to Young Ladies, on Their First Establishment in The World,* by the Dowager Countess of Carlisle, who, we learn from her forthright Introduction, had in mind a much broader audience-in-need. Also, while exerting a flourishing rhetoric, her messages were eminently more succinct. They deserve — for reasons perhaps beyond those of the Dowager — a reading in our day.

Only a very few copies of that book are extant. One is in the Rare Book Department of the Philadelphia Free Library, from which selections for this edition, with kind permission, were taken.

The author's full name was Isabella (Byron) Howard Carlisle. For easier reading, her maxims as they appear here have been somewhat reclassified and rearranged, but never rewritten.

Introduction

I UNDERTAKE this little work under the supposition that those for whose benefit I write it have been well educated. If it shall fall into the hands of such as are unblessed with this advantage, I will still presume to hope the counsels it contains may in some degree correct, if not totally eradicate, such errors as are the fruits of early neglect. On the other hand, those to whom their parents, guardians or distant relations shall have acquitted themselves of this first of important duties, will find my precepts more easy to pursue.

The subject has been so frequently and so ably treated, I am conscious that with inferior talents it carries an appearance of temerity in me to attempt to point out something new in so beaten a path of instruction. But it is my intention to treat of such minute follies and blemishes, on the first entrance of young ladies into the great and critical world, as are the less avoidable, as their consequences do not strike at first sight. There are, among these mistakes (they do not all merit a sharper epithet), some so blended with engaging qualities that they too often attract and dazzle the eyes of innocence, so as to excite a desire of imitation; and thus, by their pleasing but false colours, insensibly prove dangerous and fatal examples.

These maxims have been written at different periods, and were originally destined for the perusal of a few, either relations or acquaintances, on whose indulgence I presumed to depend; beyond that line they may appear frivolous, but experience and observation have taught me that every species of affectation, awkward habits and even involuntary omissions, when cast up by the strict hand of censure and nice criticism, have so swelled the account that persons guilty of no capital indiscretion have been, in the decline of youth and its attendant charms, treated with a severity unexpected by those accustomed to a kindness that beauty, prosperity and fashion had obtained from the public.

The Dowager Countess of Carlisle
1790

MAXIMS
Addressed to
YOUNG LADIES
On Their First Establishment in the World

Upon Entering the Marital State

Habituate yourself to that way of life most agreeable to the person to whom you are united.

Make choice of such amusements as will attach him to your company; study such occupations as will render you of consequence to him — such as the management of his fortune, and the conduct of his house — yet without assuming a superiority unbecoming of your sex.

Should he be neglectful of his family interests, supply his place with redoubled attention.

If he is misled by pleasures or hurried by passion, let not your impatience prevent his return to reason.

Let an early examination of his temper prepare

you to bear with inequalities, to which all are more or less subject.

Do not attempt to destroy his innocent pleasures by pretexts of economy; retrench rather your own expenses, to promote them.

Should he sometimes delight in trivial occupations, treat such with complaisance, as few but the idle rich have leisure to be very ill-tempered.

Disturb not the hours he may have allotted for amusement with the recital of domestic grievances.

If absolute necessity, or free choice, call him often from home (suppose it to be too often), when he shall re-visit that home, make it so agreeable that it shall finally acquire the preference.

Show the greatest respect to his near relations;

observe a constant civility towards the more distant. Let there be no marked distinction between these, on either side, in your own breast. Natural affection may, nay ought to prevail.

Let your attentions be accompanied by no affectation, yet so easy as may prove they flow from the heart.

The least appearance of flattery, mingled with assiduity, conveys a suspicion of interest.

During the education of men in schools, colleges, academies, friendships are formed, perhaps too early sometimes to be judicious, but equally hard to dissolve. If in consequence you behold such with pain, do not attempt to break them with precipitation.

When a person shall see his friends cooly received in his own house, he will naturally seek occasions to meet them abroad. Maintain therefore your interest with them, by a polite behaviour to those he so prefers, though you may not.

Unbounded demonstrations of tenderness, though authorized by sacred ties, are oft as productive of inconveniencies as the most unwarrantable aversions.

Should you have too just cause for suspicion of a change of affection, and its diversion to another object, let a ready and obliging indulgence attempt the work of reformation; it promises better success than discontent and clamorous grief.

Jealousy is capricious, its dictates inconsiderate, its suggestions fatal to mutual repose.

The allowed superiority of the other sex — the

liberties of their education — demand abundance of allowances from ours, if we aspire at esteem and influence.

The most dangerous position for a young person to be thrown into is for the world to be apprized of her harsh treatment; it exposes her to every mode of seduction that interested pity can devise, and requires infinite virtue and fortitude to guard her against its insinuations.

Should your union be attended with greater felicity than is the usual lot of our sex, govern your just affections to preserve it; by too much anxiety, you may destroy it.

If afflicted with bad health, avoid complaint; it is an increasing habit, affording no essential relief to the sufferer and apt to make the lives of others as irksome as your own.

You will contract indelicacy by description of your infirmities. You may perhaps excite compassion from an humane disposition, but you risk a dimunition of affection.

The satisfaction of those on whom you depend requires now and then some degree of self-denial in you. Amongst the happiest connections there will be diversity of opinions; and it has of old been decreed that those of the female part of the creation should give way to their superiors.

Whatever dissentions may arise, how much soever your conduct and understanding may justify the part you take in them, suffer the interference of no third person, especially if you suppose their partiality would lead them to decide in your favour.

Upon Personal Behavior

Neatness and elegance should be joined to each other; ostentation and profusion are in general equally united, and equally to be avoided.

Avoid whispering in mixed societies. It is alarming to the suspicious, mortifying to the humble, and, in itself, a habit of great impropriety.

Loud speaking and excessive laughter, the latter either pointed or unmeaning, are both unbecoming. These unguarded customs, contracted among intimates, are never pardoned by the world.

Assume no masculine airs. To support necessary fatigue is meritorious, but real robustness is denied you by nature — its semblance denied you by the laws of decency.

On no occasion relax in the article of cleanliness regarding your own person, nor suffer indolence or sickness to destroy a habit, which is as much connected with health as it is with decorum.

With regard to dress, do not aspire to be a leader in fashions, nor excessive in point of ornament.

Follow fashions at a moderate distance. Do not blindly adopt such as may expose you to ridicule, for servile imitation makes no distinctions.

Age, beauty and fortune should be such as to make the same ornaments suitable to different persons. Pursue therefore your own path of propriety, and consult your reason more than your glass.

Give up every favourite opinion, in point of dress, to that of those whom it is your duty to please.

While young, you have little need of ornaments; when old, they are ineffectual.

Attempt not to attract the eye of the public by singularity; censure will silence applause, however flattery may have encouraged you in the enterprise.

Those of our sex endowed with rare talents are sometimes too negligent of personal advantages. Science and neatness are no natural opponents.

A superior understanding will exclude the little vanities habitual to our sex.

Should those you are the most intimate with fall inadvertently into mistakes that may expose their dress or manner to ridicule, it will be as kind to give them private admonition as it would be inhuman to join in the public censure.

Upon Public Behavior

Be neither vain of your birth nor your present rank. They are accidents, not always acquired by merit; perhaps, in time, to be lamented.

Give no one, by arrogance or ill-timed haughtiness, title to enquire into your origin.

Guard your tongue and your pen against bitterness, above all when the object may ever have offended you.

The strongest proof we can give of the excellency of our principles is the pardon for injuries, as it is that of our victory over our passions.

Upon Matters of the Romantic

Romances of a moral tendency may not prove unuseful, in their effects on a mind fatigued by unavoidable application.

An excessive love of romance will make you expect to lead the life of one, and will place common cares too low in your estimation for you to attend to them.

A melancholy turn may render the tragic muse grateful to such sensations, but it is dangerous to indulge it too far, unless accompanied by religious submission.

There have been, and there still exist, many sensible persons who lead the life of romance, that can stoop to no vulgar cares. But you will, by pursuing such, hurt your fortune, neglect your children, and finally risk to be awakened from your fairy dream by some sad but common event.

Upon Beauty

During youth, be cautious of your manner of speaking of the beauty of your own sex; of its characters, when you grow old.

Should heaven have bestowed much personal perfection on you, take redoubled care of your mind.

Consider a more than ordinary share of beauty rather as a trial than a gift.

Exert your candor and show your compassion towards those whose beauty may have exposed them to error and misfortunes.

Call on your pride to suppress those emotions of envy that charity cannot conquer.

Reflect on the perpetual vicissitudes which the most beautiful, the most prosperous are subject to; you will soon exchange the look of disdain for that of pity, and the murmurs of comparison for expressions of gratitude, on your security from similar accidents.

Shut your eyes to the personal blemishes of your acquaintance, and open your ear to the sound of their virtue.

A beauty, with some share of talents, is apt to persuade herself that her arguments will prove as irresistible as her eyes, and that teasing will lose the appearance of importunity in those of an admirer. If the gaze succeeds but once, she will soon be convinced how dangerous the repetition will prove.

Upon Benevolence

Should there, among your connections, be someone, from inevitable and remote causes, plunged into distress, even from misconduct, deny yourself a superfluous ornament privately, to relieve them.

Should a plentiful fortune enable you to indulge a disposition to give, complete the happiness of the receivers by the manner of bestowing.

If ever you should have been a sufferer from ingratitude (and who has not, more or less?), do not permit the recollection to harden your heart.

Do not expect an equivalent for a kindness where there shall be the means, for generosity ceases to merit the name if it is to become an exchange.

Upon Personal Values and Pursuits

If ambitiously disposed, turn that passion towards the improvement of your mind. Every other motion will end in disappointment.

If envy, pride, severity, or a lurking love of the world's amusements haunt your solitude, your vocation is false.

Avoid the raptures and prejudices which are sometimes the attendant follies on an unbounded love of music.

It will not degrade you if you modestly interrogate those whose characters for learning and principle are established in the world. Lights from such will clear your way in the path of knowledge.

Rather prefer some hours of solitude to passing

them with a set of people who would either despise your regularity or, by forcing you out of it, destroy your happiness.

Receive your inferior neighbours with good humour and complacency; neither sigh nor sicken at conversation that situation must furnish.

Avoid the exclamations and gestures of joy or sorrow, so common at the card table, and so ridiculous to the uninterested spectator.

Curiosity is a foible, I fear, not unjustly attributed to our sex. While it remains merely as a guide in the road of instruction, it is useful, but when stretched into an impertinent enquiry, it is odious.

When you discover a studied intention to conceal events and their causes from you, be assured

it proceeds from a suspicion of your indiscretion.

Endeavour to correct a disposition to absense of mind. Its effects are various — some amusing, some ridiculous, but all unprofitable.

Your health, your spirits and your interests will all finally be sufferers by the fashionable habit of keeping late hours.

When you shall rise in a morning, with strength of body and an unrepenting heart, you will be amply recompensed for your resistance to fashion, and for having been one of the earliest in quitting the ball, or the card table.

Let your prayers be humble, short, but energetic.

Upon Presumed Knowledge of the World

Avoid warmth on political subjects; however clear your judgment, your sex is a bar to the belief of it.

Party (politics) fascinates the eyes and prejudices the understandings even of men; but partialities in our sex will be attributed to want of education and discernment.

Experience in the use of drugs may much contribute to the safety of the poor, above all, those who have slight indispositions; but a smattering in physic is rather a dangerous tool in female hands.

If possessed of a certain facility in the acquirement of language or science, avoid an impertinent display of knowledge.

Adapt your studies to your circumstances. There are some attended with much expense, and which may cause your family to lament your knowledge.

Throw not away your time on metaphysics. Your faith once settled, let no specious fabulist shake it.

Upon Regard for the Elderly

Observe a constant respect towards the advanced in age; excuse their infirmities, indulge their fancies, and mitigate the pains of decay.

Bear no harsh expression to mark your impatience occasioned by the misapprehension of decayed faculties.

Do not consider, during your youth, the aged as distinct beings from yourself; your journey, if you live, will be more speedy than you imagine, to the same period, and render you equally dependent on the compassion and patience of a younger race.

Upon Friendships

Do not permit your nearest intimates to disturb your peace at home, by oblique insinuations. Check their first approaches with severity, or slight them by silence.

Female friendships are but too frequently bars to domestic peace. They are more formed by the communication of mutual errors than the desire of amending them.

Endeavour to obtain a clear insight into the character of those persons of your sex whose exterior may incline you to wish to be connected with them, before you engage in unlimited confidence.

The friendships between two very young women, early produced in the theatre of the great world, and with both equally engaged in all the frivolities of fashion, are usually but slightly cemented, and are as briefly dissolved.

In the choice of a friend, prefer a person less young than yourself; her experience will supply your ignorance, and a single word of seasonable advice screen you from the blame of multitudes.

If your friendship can hold against the superiority of beauty and talents, that friendship will deserve its name.

Unbounded confidences are, in general, better avoided; but if you be entrusted with important secrets, endure every reproach, even the world's censure, rather than reveal them.

Listen neither to the suggestions of pleasure nor interest, where the felicity or security of a friend is concerned.

Upon Regulating Oneself

A good manager and a notable woman proves but too often to be a very unpleasant being in society. These duties should be performed in the circle of their own domestic sphere, and are never to be boasted of out of it.

Suffer not avaricious principles to deceive you in the shape of economy, nor a desire of augmenting your fortune to render you oppressive.

The luxury of this age exacts from the mistress of a great house, or indeed a smaller, some attention to a table. Disdain not therefore to give a proper application to that study.

Upon Matters of Memory

Rest not contented with the plea of a bad memory; it is but another name for negligence, among young persons.

If you venture to hazard your opinions on past events, be sure of the dates and names, for inaccuracies in these are mistakes imputed to our sex.

An exact memory will screen you from public ridicule or anger, by making you silent on particular occurrences — or keep your place, if you have any, or prevent your encroachments on that of those who are superior to you.

You should apply to the succour of memory, when trouble inclines you to fix your eye too closely on the present.

A female traveller should be doubly cautious in the communication her memory may urge her to make of her observations, as the minutest mistakes in geography, ancient history, etc. will expose her to just, though perhaps envious criticism.

To preserve a memory long, good hours are requisite, for its decay usually keeps pace with that of the body.

Upon Attending The Theatre

Refuse not to join in the general praise of those whose talents have been devoted to the entertainment of the public; though your single suffrage may prove of little weight, added to that of the multitude it will at least imply an humane intention.

Beware of bestowing public applause only by attention and smiles; it is the province of the other sex to declare their sentiments by acclamation.

If the love of admiration in your youthful days shall bear no part in your attachment to the amusements of the theatre, there are none more instructive, none more eligible for relaxation.

When you can fix your mind of the scenes before you, when the eye shall not wander to — nor the heart flutter at — the surrounding objects of the spectacle, you will return home instructed and improved.

The great utilities you may reap from well-acted tragedy are: the exciting of your compassion to real sufferings, the suppression of your vanity in prosperity, and the inspiring of you with heroic patience in adversity.

In comedy you will receive continual correction, delicately applied to your errors and foibles. Be impartial in the application, and divide it humbly with your acquaintance and friends, and even your enemies.

Further Reflections Upon Comportment in Society

In mixed conversation, do not engross more than a small portion of it.

Adapt your discourse to that of your company.

To be exact in the rules of good breeding is, in the eyes of fools of fashion, deemed awkwardness and ignorance. Sustain these interpretations without emotion, and persist intrepidly with your usual politeness, to keep impertinence at a distance.

In no other light but that of decency and modesty, at public diversions, seek to be conspicuous.

Permit no foolish insinuations or ill-bred examples ever to involve you in the disgrace of improper behavior in public or in private.

Weary not the ears of your society with the recapitulation of your own losses, and the mistakes of your partners.

Do not embitter the cheerfulness of conversation by gloomy reflections.

Whether from momentary or lasting causes you labour under uneasiness of mind, society must not share it.

In addressing parents or others of your relations, mingle your expressions of duty and regard with as much ease as they will admit of.

In answering a letter of insult or provocation, be sure of possessing yourself before you reply; for a rash expression may rise one day in judgment against you, even when you have forgotten the quarrel and the cause.

Upon the Relating to Others

Let no indirect adulation involve you in any singularity of dress, manners or opinions; the first who would thus mislead you will be the first to ridicule you in future.

It is more advantageous to live with our superiors or equals than with those of an inferior class, it being less the interest of such to flatter our foibles.

Conceal, from the indifferent spectator, the secret springs which move, regulate and perfect the arrangements of your household.

Obstinacy in dispute becomes habitual; beware of it. It will insensibly degenerate into passion, and passion degrades a woman.

Upon the Passing of Leisure

Let nothing termed diversion absorb all your leisure; it will pall finally on your taste, and become insipid from frequency.

A degree of knowledge in gardening and farming, with due attention to economy, will save you from weariness of mind, and preserve your health of body.

Upon Aging

Let each year which shall steal a charm or a grace, the companions of your youth, add a virtue in return.

The decay of beauty is perhaps one of the most sensible trials that female temper can experience. Endeavour early to prevent its consequences, by throwing your thoughts on mental acquirements.

If you desire to continue agreeably in the world, in the latter season of your life, rather promote than restrain the innocent amusements of younger persons, that the echo of cheerfulness may reach your ears.

Substitute extreme neatness to ornament; in advanced age, gentleness to vivacity, humility to vanity.

Let those hands, once perhaps too much occupied in arranging and placing personal ornament, busy themselves in forming raiment for the poor; in spinning and knitting for such ends, consolatory reflections will attend your labors.

Upon Misfortune, Illness and Death

To young persons, the death of contemporaries is the most speaking lesson they can receive.

During such afflictions as are confined to yourself, seek not relief from the dissipated and unfeeling world; nor, till you can control your sorrows, expose them to insensibility or derision.

You will meet, among indifferent spectators of misfortune, a certain hard and prying look, which seems to seek for such causes of it as may save their compassion and authorize their censure.

To wish for a cessation of pain, or mental misery, is surely allowable; but it is presumption to use importunity in requesting it.

Spare the deceased of your acquaintance your resentment, even if, during their lives, they may have merited it.

Collect together each virtue of the dead, and when the remembrance of their faults will arise, think of your own.

That natural repugnance which attends the thoughts of death has surely been implanted in our minds in order to inspire us with prudent care in the conduct of our lives. Accompany your attention to the one, by a calm submission to the other.

If your strength of mind subsists during your malady, if it gives you time for the exertion of rational power, let it check, as much as possible, those encroaching indulgencies which sickness is prone to exact.

Be assured that when able to exert your cheerfulness, it is in no wise contrary to the precepts of religion.

Fix your eye habitually on immortality, to pass more lightly through the pangs of mortality.

A continued and humble resignation will secure your peace in the most awful of moments, that of your dissolution.